Just DESSERTS

Whatever name you know them by – desserts, afters, puddings – you can bet your sweet life that there will always be a demand for creamy confections or fresh fruit dishes to round off a memorable meal. From family favourites like Plum Fritters or Treacle Tart to elaborate concoctions designed for dinner party entertaining, Just Desserts *is precisely that: a collection of recipes for all occasions, purses and preferences.*

When selecting a dessert recipe, it is important to bear in mind the dishes that will precede it. A rich main course demands to be followed by something light and easy to digest; a fruit jelly perhaps, or a sorbet or yogurt ice. Serve a simple salad as the main attraction, however, and the dessert can be as richly elaborate as you care to make it.

If the party is relatively large – a dinner for eight or more – it is customary to offer a choice of desserts. For those who take the view that a little of what they fancy is bound to do them good, Chocolate Mousse with Hazelnut Meringue might well prove popular, while guests with more self-control might prefer the refreshing Orange Terrine. Don't count on it though – in reality, most guests will try both puddings, singly or together, for there are few easier ways of sabotaging willpower than the sight of a sumptuous sweet.

CONTENTS

CUSTARDS AND CREAMS

Some of the smoothest, most sophisticated desserts come into this category. Chilled soufflés, romantic ricotta hearts, melt-in-the-mouth mousses – these are the sweets you'll always have room for.

Brandy Custard with Red Fruits

500ml (16fl oz) milk

2 eggs, separated, plus 1 egg yolk

250g (8oz) caster sugar

1 tblspn custard powder

2 tblspn brandy

freshly grated nutmeg

500g (1lb) mixed red berries (raspberries, strawberries, redcurrants, cranberries)

1 In a heavy-based saucepan, bring the milk to the boil over moderate heat.

2 Meanwhile, mix all the egg yolks with 185g (6oz) of the sugar in a large bowl. Stir in the custard powder. Beat with a hand-held electric mixer until thick and creamy. Still beating, add the hot milk in a steady stream.

3 Return the mixture to the clean pan; stir constantly over low heat until the custard thickens. Strain into a large jug, cover closely and set aside to cool.

4 Beat the egg whites in a grease-free bowl until stiff. Add the remaining sugar, 1 tablespoon at a time, beating after each addition.

5 Stir the brandy into the cooled custard, then fold in the egg whites until just combined. Divide the mixture between six individual soufflé or custard dishes and refrigerate for several hours. Dust with nutmeg and serve with the lightly chilled berries.
Serves 6

Chilled Passionfruit Soufflé

5 tblspn cornflour

750ml (1¼pt) milk

125g (4oz) caster sugar

2 tspn vanilla essence

1 tblspn powdered gelatine

60ml (2fl oz) water

125ml (4fl oz) single cream

1 x 170g (5½oz) can passionfruit pulp

45g (1½oz) toasted coconut

1 In a small bowl, mix the cornflour to a paste with 60ml (2fl oz) of the milk. Put the remaining milk in a saucepan. Stir in the sugar, vanilla essence and cornflour paste. Bring to the boil, stirring until the custard boils and thickens. Pour into a bowl, cover closely and set aside to cool to room temperature.

2 Dissolve the gelatine in the water (see page 5). Cool, but do not allow to set.

3 Whisk the gelatine, cream and passionfruit pulp into the cooled custard. Refrigerate for 10 minutes.

4 Lightly grease four 250ml (8fl oz) soufflé dishes. Give each a paper collar, extending 3cm (1¼in) above the rim. Divide the mixture between the dishes.

5 Refrigerate the soufflés until set. Remove the paper collars, turn the soufflés on their sides and roll them in the coconut. Decorate with strawberries and passionfruit pulp, if liked.
Serves 4

Chilled Passionfruit Soufflé

Strawberry Hearts

Strawberry Hearts

250g (8oz) strawberries, hulled and chopped

30g (1oz) icing sugar

250g (8oz) ricotta cheese

155ml (5fl oz) double cream

2 tspn powdered gelatine

60ml (2fl oz) freshly squeezed orange juice

1 Combine strawberries, icing sugar, ricotta and cream in a blender or food processor. Process until smooth.

2 Dissolve gelatine in orange juice (see page 5). Add to strawberry mixture; process for just long enough to mix.

3 Lightly grease four heart-shaped moulds. Carefully line with damp muslin. Spoon in mixture, taking care to fill all corners. Refrigerate until set. Unmould ricotta hearts onto a serving dish, removing muslin.
Serves 4

Grape Brûlée

185g (6oz) seedless green grapes, stems removed

1 egg plus 3 egg yolks

155g (5oz) caster sugar

250ml (8fl oz) double cream

3 tblspn Grand Marnier

30g (1oz) flaked almonds

2 tblspn soft brown sugar

1 Divide grapes between four individual gratin dishes.

2 Combine whole egg and egg yolks in a heatproof bowl. Add sugar and beat until thick and creamy. Place bowl over simmering water. Continue to beat, gradually adding cream and Grand Marnier, until volume increases and custard thickens.

3 Pour custard over grapes. Sprinkle with almonds and thin layer of brown sugar. Grill under moderate heat until sugar melts; serve at once.
Serves 4

Chestnut Mousse

440ml (14fl oz) milk

4 tspn powdered gelatine

60ml (2fl oz) water

3 eggs, separated, plus 1 egg yolk

60g (2oz) caster sugar

1 x 485g (15½oz) can sweetened chestnut purée

300ml (10fl oz) double cream, chilled

pinch salt

1 Bring milk to the boil in a saucepan. Cool. Sprinkle gelatine over water in a small bowl. Set aside.

2 Beat all egg yolks with sugar in a heatproof bowl until pale and light. Stir in cooled milk. Set bowl over simmering water and cook, stirring constantly, for 15 minutes, or until custard coats the back of the spoon.

3 Stir in gelatine. Strain custard into a clean bowl, cover closely. Cool then refrigerate until almost set.

4 Mash chestnut purée until smooth. Stir in custard. Beat cream until soft peaks form, then fold into custard mixture.

5 Beat egg whites and salt in a grease-free bowl until stiff peaks form. Fold egg white mixture into chestnut custard. Spoon into a serving bowl. Cover. Refrigerate until set.
Serves 8-10

Sabayon with Berries

1 tspn powdered gelatine
3 tblspn water
3 egg yolks
2 tblspn caster sugar
2 tblspn Cointreau
125ml (4fl oz) double cream
185g (6oz) strawberries, hulled and sliced
125g (4oz) blueberries
icing sugar for dusting

1 Dissolve gelatine in water (see right). Combine egg yolks, sugar and Cointreau in a heatproof bowl. Place over simmering water. Whisk mixture constantly for 3-5 minutes or until thick. Whisk in gelatine, remove from heat and continue to whisk until mixture is cool.

2 Whip cream until soft peaks form. Fold into Cointreau mixture. Divide between four dessert glasses.

3 Arrange glasses on individual plates, adding a portion of mixed berries to each. Dust berries with icing sugar.
Serves 4

Kitchen Tip
To cool the sabayon more quickly during the whisking process, place the bowl in a larger container filled with ice cubes.

Apricot Mousse

375ml (12fl oz) double cream
2 tblspn icing sugar
1 x 470g (15oz) can apricot halves, drained
1 tspn lemon juice
1 tblspn powdered gelatine
60ml (2fl oz) freshly squeezed orange juice
250g (8oz) raspberries
1 tblspn raspberry liqueur

1 In a bowl, whip cream with icing sugar until soft peaks form. Purée apricots with lemon juice in a blender or food processor until just smooth; alternatively, press through a sieve into a bowl. Fold apricot purée into cream.

2 Dissolve gelatine in orange juice (see right). Cool slightly, then stir into apricot cream. Divide mixture between six ramekins; chill until set.

3 To make coulis, press the raspberries through a sieve into a bowl. Stir in liqueur.

4 Unmould the mousses onto six individual dessert plates. Serve with the raspberry coulis.
Serves 6

Gelatine Know-How
Gelatine is an excellent setting agent and is easy to use. Always dissolve gelatine in hot liquid before use. It is usual to soften or 'sponge' the gelatine in a small amount of cold water first, then heat the mixture until completely clear. Any undissolved gelatine is liable to form unpalatable threads in the finished dessert.

Sprinkle the gelatine onto the liquid (usually water or fruit juice) in a small heatproof bowl. Set it aside for about 5 minutes until the gelatine expands and acquires a spongy appearance. Melt the gelatine either by placing the bowl in a saucepan of hot water, stirring until the gelatine dissolves, or by heating in the microwave on HIGH (100%) for about 30 seconds.

Sabayon with Berries

Floating Islands on Passionfruit and Toffee Cream

250g (8oz) caster sugar

2 tblspn redcurrant jelly

90ml (3fl oz) water

4 mint sprigs to decorate

Meringue

6 egg whites

155g (5oz) caster sugar

Passionfruit Cream

250ml (8fl oz) carton custard

125ml (4fl oz) double cream

pulp of 3 passionfruit

1 Combine the sugar, redcurrant jelly and 60ml (2fl oz) of the water in a saucepan. Stir over low heat until the sugar has dissolved, then raise the heat slightly and cook the mixture until it turns golden brown. Immediately plunge the base of the pan in cold water to prevent further cooking. Stir in the remaining water, taking care as the mixture may spit. Cool to room temperature, refrigerate for 1 hour.

2 Meanwhile, make the meringue. Beat the egg whites in a large grease-free bowl until soft peaks form. Add the sugar 1 tablespoon at a time, beating until stiff.

3 Bring a medium saucepan of water to the boil; reduce the heat to a simmer. Using 2 tablespoons, shape a little of the meringue into an oval shape.

Carefully slide it into the simmering water. Repeat the process to cook two meringues at a time, allowing 2 minutes per side. Using a slotted spoon, carefully transfer the meringues to paper towels to drain.

4 Make the passionfruit cream by mixing all the ingredients together in a bowl. Spoon a little cream onto each of four dessert plates. Drizzle the cold toffee in a thin stream over the top. Float three meringues on each portion and decorate with mint.
Serves 4

Lime and Lemon Pots

4 egg yolks

60g (2oz) caster sugar

1 tspn grated lemon rind

1 tspn grated lime rind

1 tblspn lemon juice

1 tblspn freshly squeezed lime juice

250ml (8fl oz) double cream

To Decorate

whipped cream

slivers of lime rind

1 Preheat oven to 150°C (300°F/ Gas 2). Beat the egg yolks with the sugar in a large bowl until pale and creamy. Beat in the lemon and lime rind with the combined juices. Add the cream and continue to beat for 1 minute.

2 Divide the mixture between six 125ml (4fl oz) pots or ramekins. Place the pots in a roasting tin and add boiling water to come to within 2cm (3/4in) of the tops of the pots.

3 Bake the lime and lemon pots for 40 minutes or until the custard is set. Remove from the water and cool completely.

4 Just before serving, top each pot with a swirl of whipped cream and a few slivers of lime rind.
Serves 6

Lime and Lemon Pots

Floating Islands on Passionfruit and Toffee Cream

Mango Whip

2 mangoes, peeled and stoned

1 tblspn caster sugar

1 tblspn powdered gelatine

60ml (2fl oz) water

185ml (6fl oz) evaporated milk, chilled

1 Purée mangoes in a blender or food processor. Transfer to a bowl and stir in sugar.

2 Dissolve gelatine in water (see page 5). Stir into mango mixture.

3 Whip evaporated milk until frothy; fold it into apricot mixture. Pour into four serving glasses and refrigerate until set. Decorate with sliced mango and strawberries, if liked.

Serves 4

Tea Cream Bavarois

1 tblspn powdered gelatine

60ml (2fl oz) cold water

500ml (16fl oz) milk

4 tblspn breakfast tea leaves

6 egg yolks

110g (3¹/₂oz) caster sugar

185ml (6fl oz) double cream, whipped

1 Dissolve gelatine in water (see page 5). Heat milk and tea leaves in a saucepan to just below boiling point. Meanwhile beat egg yolks with caster sugar in a large bowl until thick and creamy.

2 Strain milky tea mixture into bowl, beating constantly. Return mixture to clean pan; stir over low heat until custard thickens. Whisk in gelatine, cover custard closely and set aside to cool.

3 Fold in whipped cream. Divide mixture between six lightly oiled bavarois moulds, cover and refrigerate until set. Unmould the bavarois on dessert plates. Decorate with blueberries dusted with icing sugar, if liked.

Serves 6

Mango Whip

Crème Caramel, Tea Cream Bavarois

Crème Caramel

500g (1lb) caster sugar

250ml (8fl oz) water

8 eggs, plus 4 egg yolks

125g (4oz) icing sugar

1-1.2 litres (1³/₄-2pt) milk

2 tspn vanilla essence

1 Preheat oven to 180°C (350°F/ Gas 4). Heat caster sugar with half the water in a heavy-based saucepan, stirring until sugar has dissolved. Raise heat. Cook without stirring until golden. Pour enough of caramel into base of a 22cm (8³/₄in) round cake tin to coat bottom and sides.

2 Add rest of water to remaining caramel in pan; cook over low heat until caramel dissolves. Cool, then chill until required.

3 Whisk whole eggs, egg yolks, icing sugar, milk and vanilla until well combined. Strain mixture. Then pour carefully into caramel-lined cake tin. Place tin in a roasting tin, add boiling water to a depth of 2cm (³/₄in) and bake for 1¹/₄ hours. Remove from water, cool, then cover and refrigerate overnight.

4 To serve, run a knife along inner edge of custard to loosen. Turn onto a serving platter. Decorate with reserved caramel sauce.

Serves 8

CRÊPES, FRITTERS AND BLINIS

Its a toss up who likes crêpes best – children or adults. One thing is for certain: the sight of any batch of batter, whether it be for blinis, fritters, pancakes or sweet soufflés, will bring smiles to the faces of the family.

Banana Fritters with Vanilla Sauce

6 bananas

oil for deep frying

Batter

90ml (3fl oz) milk

125ml (4fl oz) single cream

90g (3oz) self-raising flour

60g (2oz) cornflour

¼ tspn ground cloves

Vanilla Sauce

125g (4oz) butter

250g (8oz) soft brown sugar

125ml (4fl oz) single cream

1 tspn vanilla essence

1 Make batter. Mix milk and cream in a jug. Combine flour, cornflour and ground cloves in a large bowl. Make a well in the centre. Add cream mixture and gradually incorporate flour to make a smooth batter.

2 Make sauce. Melt butter in a saucepan. Off heat, stir in brown sugar, cream and vanilla. Cook over low heat, stirring constantly, for 5 minutes, until all the sugar is dissolved. Do not allow sauce to boil. Set aside.

3 Cut bananas in half, dip them in batter until generously coated and deep fry in hot oil until golden. Drain on paper towels. Serve at once, decorated with fresh sliced bananas and with a little of the sauce poured over top. Offer remaining sauce separately.
Serves 6

Plum Fritters

16 firm plums

oil for deep frying

Batter

90g (3oz) self-raising flour

60g (2oz) cornflour

1 tblspn caster sugar

½ tspn ground cinnamon

215ml (7fl oz) milk

To Serve

250ml (8fl oz) carton custard

125ml (4fl oz) double cream

1 Make the batter. Combine the flour, cornflour, caster sugar and cinnamon in a large bowl. Make a well in the centre. Add the milk and gradually incorporate the flour to make a smooth batter.

2 Using a metal skewer, dip the plums in the batter, coating them well. Deep fry, four at a time, until golden. Drain on paper towels.

3 Combine the custard and cream in a small bowl. Spoon a little of the mixture onto each plate and arrange three or four plums on each. Decorate with mint sprigs and sliced fresh plums, if liked.
Serves 4-6

Banana Fritters with Vanilla Sauce, Plum Fritters

Omelette Soufflé with Strawberries

Omelette Soufflé with Strawberries

4 eggs, separated, plus 2 egg yolks

30g (1oz) caster sugar

1 tblspn vanilla essence

60ml (2fl oz) double cream

1 tspn butter

4 tblspn redcurrant jelly

1 tblspn lemon juice

375g (12oz) fresh strawberries, hulled and halved

60g (2oz) icing sugar

1 Beat all egg yolks with caster sugar until pale and creamy. Beat in vanilla and cream.

2 In a separate bowl, whisk egg whites until soft peaks form; fold into egg yolk mixture.

3 Heat a large omelette pan over moderate heat. Add butter. Pour in batter, spreading evenly with a spatula. Cook until base is set.

4 Transfer pan to a low grill and cook for 2 minutes or until set on top. Meanwhile, heat redcurrant jelly with lemon juice and strawberries in a small pan, stirring. Slide omelette onto a large platter, pile strawberry sauce over one half and flip other half over. Dust with icing sugar and serve.
Serves 4

Pecan Meringue Crêpes

375g (12fl oz) milk

2 eggs, lightly beaten

155g (5oz) self-raising flour

2 tblspn sugar

Filling

1 egg plus 2 egg whites

1 tblspn plain flour

125g (4oz) caster sugar

60g (2oz) pecan nuts, chopped

1 Preheat oven to 160°C (325°F/ Gas 3). Mix milk and eggs in a jug. Combine flour and sugar in a large bowl, make a well in centre and pour in milk mixture. Gradually mix to make a smooth batter.

2 Heat a greased crêpe pan over moderate heat. Pour in about 2 tablespoons of batter, tilting pan to cover bottom thinly. Cook until golden underneath, turn and cook other side until golden. Repeat with remaining batter to make 8-10 crêpes.

3 To make filling, beat whole egg with flour and half the caster sugar in a bowl, until thick and creamy. Stir in nuts. Whisk egg whites in a bowl until soft peaks form. Gradually add remaining caster sugar, beating until mixture is stiff. Fold in pecan mixture. Divide filling between crêpes, roll up and arrange in a greased baking dish. Bake for 20 minutes.
Serves 4-5

Blinis with Strawberries

Lemon Soufflé Omelette

2 eggs, separated

2 tblspn single cream

60g (2oz) caster sugar

1 tblspn lemon juice

1 tblspn freshly squeezed lime juice

15g (¹/₂oz) butter

icing sugar for dusting

1 Combine egg yolks, cream, caster sugar and citrus juices in a bowl. Using an electric mixer, beat for 1 minute.

2 In a separate bowl, whisk egg whites until soft peaks form. Fold egg yolk mixture into whites, one tablespoon at a time.

3 Heat an omelette pan over moderate heat. Add butter. Pour in batter, spreading it evenly with a spatula. Cook until golden underneath.

4 Transfer pan to a low grill and cook for 2 minutes more or until set. Ease omelette onto a serving plate, fold in half and dust with icing sugar. Serve.
Serves 1

Blinis with Strawberries

15g (¹/₂oz) fresh yeast

1 tspn caster sugar

250ml (8fl oz) milk, warmed

3 eggs, separated

125ml (4fl oz) soured cream

155g (5oz) plain flour

500g (1lb) strawberries, hulled and quartered

3 tblspn Cointreau

30g (1oz) butter

ice cream to serve

1 Mash yeast with sugar and warm milk in a large bowl. Set aside for 10 minutes.

2 Whisk egg yolks with soured cream in a separate bowl; stir into yeast mixture. Whisk in flour, cover with a damp tea-towel and stand in a warm place for 1 hour.

3 Meanwhile, make a sauce by puréeing half the strawberries with the Cointreau. Press through a sieve and set aside.

4 Beat egg whites in a bowl until soft peaks form. Fold into yeast mixture.

5 Heat butter in a frying pan, add tablespoons of batter to pan. Cook for 1 minute on each side. Drain on paper towels and arrange on dessert plates. Serve with remaining strawberries, ice cream. and strawberry sauce.
Serves 4

Chocolate Fritters

Chocolate Crêpes

3 eggs, lightly beaten

15g (1/2oz) butter, melted

250ml (8fl oz) milk

90g (3oz) plain flour

4 scoops chocolate ice cream

200g (61/2oz) dark chocolate, melted

125ml (4fl oz) double cream

1 tblspn Kahlua

30g (1oz) pistachio nuts, chopped

1 Combine eggs, butter and milk. Place flour in a bowl, make a well in the centre and pour in milk mixture. Gradually mix to make a smooth batter. Cover and stand for 30 minutes.

2 Heat a greased crêpe pan. Pour in about 2 tablespoons of batter, tilting pan to cover bottom thinly. Cook over moderate heat until golden underneath, turn and cook other side until golden. Repeat with remaining batter to make 8 crêpes. Fold crêpes into triangles and place two on each dessert plate. Add a scoop of ice cream.

3 To make sauce, combine melted chocolate, cream and Kahlua. Pour sauce over crêpes, sprinkle with chopped nuts.
Serves 4

Chocolate Fritters

125g (4oz) chocolate cake crumbs

1 tblspn cocoa

155g (5oz) dark chocolate, melted

2 tblspn double cream

Batter

90g (3oz) self-raising flour

45g (11/2oz) custard powder

1/4 tspn ground cinnamon

185-215ml (6-7fl oz) milk

oil for deep frying

1 Process cake crumbs, cocoa, chocolate and cream in a blender or food processor until smooth. Press over base of a lined and greased 18cm (7in) square cake tin. Freeze for 2 hours.

2 Make batter. Combine flour, custard powder and cinnamon in a bowl, make a well in the centre, add 185ml (6fl oz) of milk and gradually mix to a smooth batter. Add remaining milk if required; the batter should be of a thick coating consistency. Cover. Chill until required.

3 Cut chocolate mixture into about 12 triangles. Dip in batter. Deep fry in hot oil until golden brown, drain on paper towels and serve.
Makes about 12

Chocolate Crêpes

CHOCOHOLIC'S CHOICE

*The desserts most in demand, on trolley or buffet table, invariably contain chocolate.
This chapter includes old favourites like chocolate mousse and brownies, and introduces
some fresh ideas for this perennially popular ingredient.*

Chocolate Mousse with Hazelnut Meringue

6 egg whites

250g (8oz) caster sugar

125g (4oz) hazelnuts, ground

Mousse

250ml (8fl oz) carton custard

125ml (4fl oz) double cream

155g (5oz) dark chocolate, melted

2 tblspn Kahlua

2 tspn powdered gelatine

60ml (2fl oz) water

sifted cocoa, whipped cream and sliced strawberries, to decorate

1 Preheat oven to 150°C (300°F/ Gas 2). Beat the egg whites in a large grease-free bowl until soft peaks form. Gradually add the sugar, beating constantly until the mixture is stiff. Gently fold in the hazelnuts until well combined.

2 Divide mixture between two lined and greased 20cm (8in) round cake tins. Bake for 1 hour or until golden. Cool on wire racks.

3 Meanwhile make mousse. Beat custard, cream, chocolate and Kahlua in a bowl. Dissolve gelatine in water (see page 5). Stir into chocolate mixture. Chill for 1 hour or until mousse is thick enough to hold its shape.

4 Spread mousse over one meringue round; top with other. Dust with cocoa and decorate with whipped cream and strawberries.
Serves 6

Chocolate Mousse with Hazelnut Meringue, Chocolate Mille Feuilles with Raspberries

Chocolate Mille Feuilles with Raspberries

315g (10oz) dark chocolate, in squares

1 tblspn powdered gelatine

60ml (2fl oz) water

250ml (8fl oz) carton custard

1 tspn vanilla essence

60ml (2fl oz) double cream

155g (5oz) white chocolate, melted

185g (6oz) raspberries

1 Melt the dark chocolate in a heatproof bowl over hot water. Thinly spread an even layer of chocolate over two 20 x 13cm (8 x 5in) pieces of nonstick baking parchment supported on baking sheets. Refrigerate until set.

2 Dissolve gelatine in water (see page 5).

3 Using a hand-held electric mixer, beat the custard, vanilla and cream in a bowl until combined. Continue to beat while adding the melted white chocolate. Beat in the gelatine; chill until on the point of setting.

4 Using a sharp knife dipped in hot water, cut the set chocolate into eight 10 x 6cm (4 x 2½in) rectangles; carefully peel off the paper. Place one chocolate rectangle on each serving plate.

5 Stir the mousse; it should be very thick. Spoon a layer of mousse onto each chocolate rectangle, add a layer of raspberries and top with a second chocolate rectangle. Serve.
Serves 4

Dark Chocolate Bavarois

250ml (8fl oz) milk

4 egg yolks

60g (2oz) caster sugar

2 tspn powdered gelatine

60ml (2fl oz) water

200g (6½oz) dark chocolate, melted

440ml (14fl oz) double cream

100g (3½oz) white chocolate, grated

1 Scald the milk in a medium saucepan. Beat the egg yolks with the sugar in a bowl until pale. While beating, add the hot milk. Return the mixture to the clean pan and stir over low heat until the custard thickens slightly.

2 Dissolve the gelatine in the water (see page 5). Remove the custard from the heat; stir in the gelatine and melted dark chocolate. Cool for 10 minutes.

3 Beat 250ml (8fl oz) of the cream in a bowl until soft peaks form. Fold it into the chocolate mixture, divide between four lightly greased 250ml (8fl oz) moulds; chill until set.

4 Make a sauce by heating the white chocolate with the remaining cream. Stir, then cool to room temperature. Serve the mousses on dessert plates, with the sauce.
Serves 4

Mocha Cream Pots

6 egg yolks

90g (3oz) soft brown sugar

375ml (12fl oz) single cream

125ml (4fl oz) milk

2 tblspn instant coffee

2 tblspn cocoa

60ml (2fl oz) hot water

raspberries and mint leaves to decorate

1 Preheat oven to 180°C (350°F/ Gas 4). Mix the egg yolks with half the brown sugar in a medium bowl. Using a hand-held electric mixer, beat the mixture for 1 minute.

2 Combine the cream, milk and remaining sugar in a small saucepan. Bring to the boil over low heat, stirring constantly.

3 Mix the coffee and cocoa in a small jug. Add the hot water, stirring the mocha mixture until smooth.

4 Remove the cream mixture from the heat; whisk in the mocha mixture until dissolved. Gradually whisk this mixture into the egg yolks.

5 Divide the mixture between six pots or eight ramekins. Place in a deep roasting tin and add boiling water to a depth of 4cm (1½in).

6 Cover the dish with foil. Bake for 30-35 minutes. Remove the pots or ramekins from the water. When cool, refrigerate until required. Just before serving, decorate the desserts with raspberries and mint leaves. Serve with dessert biscuits, if liked.

Serves 6-8

Variation

For plain chocolate cream pots, omit the coffee and use 3 tablespoons of cocoa. Add 1 teaspoon chocolate liqueur and decorate the pots or ramekins with chocolate caraque.

Chocolate Soufflé

Chocolate Soufflé

110g (3¹/₂oz) dark chocolate

370ml (12fl oz) hot milk

30g (1oz) butter

2 tblspn plain flour

¹/₂ tspn vanilla essence

3 eggs, separated

60g (2oz) caster sugar

icing sugar for dusting

1 Preheat oven to 180°C (350°F/ Gas 4). Melt the chocolate, see Kitchen Tip. Stir in 60ml (2fl oz) of the hot milk until well combined; set aside.

2 Melt the butter in a saucepan over moderate heat. Stir in the flour and cook for 1 minute. Gradually add the remaining milk, stirring until the mixture boils and thickens. Remove from the heat and stir in the vanilla.

3 Beat the egg yolks, one at a time, into chocolate mixture. Add the caster sugar and beat well. Stir the mixture into the hot white sauce.

4 In a large grease-free bowl, whisk the egg whites until soft peaks form. Fold in the chocolate sauce, a little at a time.

5 Lightly grease eight individual soufflé dishes. Divide the mixture between the dishes, filling them three quarters of the way up. Bake for 25 minutes or until the soufflés are well risen and firm to the touch. Dust the tops with icing sugar and serve.
Serves 8

Kitchen Tip
Chocolate should be melted over moderate, not high heat. One of the best ways to do this is to bring a small saucepan of water to the boil. Remove the pan from the heat and place a heatproof bowl containing the chocolate (broken into squares) on top of it. The bowl should not be in contact with the water. When the chocolate is melted, stir it lightly.

Mocha Cream Pots

White Chocolate Mousse

200g (6¹/₂oz) white chocolate, in squares

60ml (2fl oz) double cream

60g (2oz) butter, softened

3 eggs, separated

75g (2¹/₂oz) dark chocolate

1 Combine white chocolate and cream in a heatproof bowl. Bring a saucepan of water to boil, remove from heat and place bowl on top. When chocolate softens, stir it into cream.

2 Beat butter and egg yolks into chocolate mixture. Return pan to heat. When water simmers, replace bowl. Cook, stirring constantly, until mixture thickens. Cool.

3 Beat egg whites in a grease-free bowl until stiff; fold into the chocolate mixture. Divide between four serving glasses and chill until set.

4 Melt dark chocolate and drizzle a design on each dessert; return to refrigerator until required. Serve decorated with strawberries if liked.

Serves 4

White Chocolate Mousse

Chocolate Almond Slices

185g (6oz) flaked almonds, roughly chopped

75g (2¹/₂oz) plain flour

155g (5oz) milk chocolate, chopped

60g (2oz) butter, melted

2 large eggs

75g (2¹/₂oz) caster sugar

185g (6oz) golden syrup

Topping

155g (5oz) dark chocolate

45g (1¹/₂oz) butter

1 Preheat oven to 180°C (350°F/Gas 4). Combine almonds and flour in a large bowl. Grease and base-line a 20cm (8in) square cake tin. Melt chocolate, see Kitchen Tip, page 19; stir in butter.

2 In a separate bowl, beat eggs with sugar until pale and thick; beat in syrup with melted chocolate and butter, then stir in almond mixture.

3 Spoon mixture into prepared tin. Bake for 30 minutes. Cool.

4 For topping, melt chocolate and butter together. Mix well; spread over cooled cake. Slice when the chocolate has set.

Makes about 18

Choc-mint Brownies

125g (4oz) butter

200g (6¹/₂oz) dark chocolate, grated

2 eggs

140g (4¹/₂oz) soft brown sugar

2 tblspn cocoa

2 tblspn oil

125g (4oz) plain flour

Icing

15g (¹/₂oz) butter, softened

140g (4¹/₂oz) icing sugar

3 drops peppermint essence

1 Preheat oven to 150°C (300°F/ Gas 2). Melt butter with the chocolate in a heatproof bowl set over simmering water; cool slightly. Combine eggs and sugar in a bowl. Beat with a hand-held electric mixer until pale and creamy. Beat in cocoa and oil, then gradually add flour and cooled chocolate mixture, beating frequently.

2 Pour mixture into a lined and greased 20cm (8in) square cake tin. Bake for 40 minutes. Turn onto a wire rack to cool.

3 Make icing. Beat butter with icing sugar in a bowl. Add essence and a few drops of water. Mix to a smooth pouring consistency.

4 Drizzle icing over top of cake. When set, cut into 16 brownies.
Makes 16

Cheats' Chocolate Cake

1 packet rich chocolate cake mix
30g (1oz) hazelnuts, very finely chopped
45g (1½oz) soft brown sugar
250g (8oz) strawberries, hulled
1 tblspn strawberry jam
1 tblspn lemon juice
2 tspn single cream
strawberries to decorate

1 Preheat oven and make up chocolate cake mix according to package instructions.

2 Line and grease a loaf tin. Mix chopped hazelnuts and brown sugar in a bowl; sprinkle mixture evenly over base of tin.

3 Spoon cake mixture into tin, taking care not to disturb nut mixture. Bake according to package instructions. Cool on a wire rack.

4 Purée strawberries with jam and lemon juice in a blender or food processor until smooth. Press sauce through a sieve into a jug. Pour a little sauce onto each dessert plate, add a slice of cake and drip three drops of cream onto sauce. Draw a toothpick through cream. Decorate with fresh strawberries.
Serves 6

Cheats' Chocolate Cake

Fruit Favourites

After a rich main course, what better way to cleanse the palate than with a refreshing fruit dessert such as Jewelled Jelly, Orange Terrine or simple Baked Peaches with Custard?

Jewelled Jelly with Apricot Sauce

2 tspn powdered gelatine
1 x 90g (3oz) packet blackcurrant jelly crystals
250ml (8fl oz) water
5 tblspn sweet white wine
2 tblspn lemon juice
750ml (1¼pt) apple juice
280g (9oz) strawberries, hulled and sliced
4 kiwi fruit, peeled and sliced

Sauce

250g (8oz) apricots, pitted and chopped
4 tblspn apricot jam
300ml (10fl oz) water

1 Dissolve gelatine and jelly crystals in water (see page 5). Combine wine, lemon juice, apple juice and jelly/gelatine mixture in a bowl, stir well and set aside.

2 Lightly oil a 1.5 litre (2½pt) jelly mould. Arrange half the strawberries and kiwifruit in the mould, gently pour over half the jelly mixture and chill until set.

3 Arrange remaining fruit on set jelly, carefully pour over the remaining liquid jelly and refrigerate for several hours until set.

4 Meanwhile make sauce by heating apricots with jam and water in a small saucepan. Simmer for 5 minutes, press mixture through a sieve into a bowl and serve with jelly.

Serves 6

Summer Pudding

10 slices day-old white bread, crusts removed
3 tblspn milk
750g (1½lb) mixed soft fruit (raspberries, strawberries, redcurrants and blackcurrants)
100g (3½oz) caster sugar

1 Lightly grease a 1 litre (1¾pt) pudding basin. Cut the bread into fingers, 3cm (1¼in) wide; moisten with the milk.

2 Combine the fruit and sugar in a large saucepan. Bring to the boil over low heat, stirring lightly from time to time to dissolve the sugar. Lower the heat and simmer for 5 minutes. Pour off one third of the juice and set aside in a jug. Cool the fruit and remaining juice.

3 Line pudding basin with bread slices, reserving enough bread for the top. Spoon fruit into mould; cover closely with reserved bread. Cover with a plate or saucer that fits basin exactly and add a weight to compress pudding. Refrigerate overnight.

4 Invert pudding on a serving plate. Pour reserved juice over to cover any places where juices have not seeped through. Serve at once.

Serves 4

Jewelled Jelly with Apricot Sauce

Baked Peaches

Baked Peaches

4 peaches, skinned, halved and stoned

185ml (6fl oz) Amaretto (almond liqueur)

125g (4oz) caster sugar

185ml (6fl oz) double cream

2 tspn brandy

185ml (6fl oz) carton custard

185g (6oz) blackcurrants

1 tblspn soft brown sugar

2 tblspn water

1 Preheat oven to 180°C (350°F/ Gas 4). Place peaches cut side down in a baking dish. Pour over liqueur and sprinkle with caster sugar, bake for 30 minutes.

2 Combine cream, brandy and custard. Spoon a puddle of sauce onto bottom of each dessert plate.

3 Simmer blackcurrants with brown sugar and water until sugar dissolves. Press through a sieve. Chill.

4 Place two baked peach halves in centre of each custard puddle, spoon a little almond liqueur syrup over top

5 Dot blackcurrant purée around edge of each plate. Drag a toothpick through dots to form hearts.
Serves 4

Oranges in Red Wine

500ml (18fl oz) red wine

4 tblspn redcurrant jelly

125g (4oz) caster sugar

4 large navel oranges, segmented

Combine wine, jelly and sugar in a saucepan. Bring to boil, stirring, then lower heat and simmer for 10 minutes or until syrup thickens slightly. Arrange orange segments in heatproof glasses, pour over hot wine syrup and serve.
Serves 4

Oranges in Red Wine

Pear Soufflé

45g (1¹/₂oz) butter

3 tblspn plain flour

375ml (12fl oz) hot milk

125g (4oz) caster sugar

1 x 470g (15oz) can pears, drained

2 tblspn lemon juice

3 eggs, separated

1 Preheat oven to 180°C (350°F/ Gas 4). Grease a 1 litre (1³/₄pt) soufflé dish. Fit a paper collar, extending 3cm (1¹/₄in) above rim. Melt butter in a saucepan over moderate heat. Stir in flour. Cook for 1 minute. Gradually add hot milk and sugar, stirring until sauce boils and thickens. Remove from heat, cover closely and cool to room temperature.

2 Purée pears with lemon juice in a blender or food processor; stir into sauce. Whisk in egg yolks.

3 Beat egg whites in a bowl until soft peaks form. Fold into pear sauce mixture. Pour mixture into prepared soufflé dish. Bake for 35 minutes or until well risen.

Serves 4

Pear Soufflé

Apricot Meringue

1 x 822g (1lb 10oz) can apricots, drained

2 tblspn brandy

1 tspn vanilla essence

3 eggs, separated

125g (4oz) caster sugar

1 Preheat oven to 180°C (350°F/ Gas 4). Purée apricots with brandy, vanilla, egg yolks and half the sugar in a blender or food processor. Pour mixture into a greased 20cm (8in) baking dish. Bake for 8 minutes, remove from oven and set aside.

2 Combine egg whites and remaining sugar in a bowl. Whisk with an electric mixer until soft peaks form. Carefully spread meringue over apricot base, swirling into peaks. Return to oven and bake for 20 minutes.

Serves 4

Apricot Meringue

Orange Terrine

2¹/₂ tblspn powdered gelatine

185ml (6fl oz) water

750ml (1¹/₄pt) apple juice

2 tblspn lemon juice

1 tblspn freshly squeezed lime juice

1 tblspn chopped fresh mint

2 oranges, segmented

375ml (12fl oz) freshly squeezed orange juice

2 tblspn Cointreau

2 tblspn grated orange rind

1 Dissolve gelatine in water (see page 5). Divide apple juice between two bowls. Add one third of the gelatine mixture to first bowl. Stir in lemon juice, lime juice and mint. Pour mixture into a lightly oiled 1 litre (1³/₄pt) loaf tin; chill until set.

2 Arrange orange segments in a row along top of the set jelly. Combine orange juice and Cointreau. Stir in half remaining gelatine mixture (warming it if it has solidified). Gently pour over back of a spoon onto oranges, taking care not to disturb the set jelly. Chill until set.

3 Stir orange rind and remaining gelatine mixture (warming it as before) into reserved apple juice. Gently pour over set orange jelly. Chill until firm.
Serves 6

Brandied Figs

8 fresh figs, halved

125ml (4fl oz) water

4 tblspn soft brown sugar

3 tblspn brandy

1 Preheat oven to 200°C (400°F/ Gas 6). Arrange figs cut side up in a single layer in a baking dish.

2 Combine water and sugar in a saucepan. Bring to the boil, stirring until sugar dissolves, then boil without stirring for 2 minutes. Stir in brandy and pour mixture over and around figs.

3 Bake figs for 20 minutes, until heated through and bubbly. Serve at once.
Serves 4

Gratin of Summer Fruits

250g (8oz) strawberries, hulled and halved

1 cantaloupe melon, halved, seeded and cubed or shaped into balls

4 peaches, skinned, halved, stoned and sliced

500g (1lb) raspberries, hulled

3 tblspn orange liqueur

juice of 1 orange

2 tblspn caster sugar plus extra for topping, see method

Sauce

6 egg yolks

5 tblspn caster sugar

1 Combine strawberries, melon balls, peaches and raspberries in a bowl. Mix gently.

2 Combine liqueur with orange juice. Stir in 2 tablespoons of sugar until dissolved. Pour mixture over fruit, cover and stand at room temperature for 1 hour.

3 Make sauce. Combine egg yolks and caster sugar in top of a double boiler. Set pan over simmering water and whisk until mixture is pale and frothy. Continue whisking until custard coats back of a spoon. Draw off about 125ml (4fl oz) of the juices from fruit bowl; gradually add to egg yolk mixture, whisking constantly.

4 Tip contents of fruit bowl into a buttered baking dish. Pour sauce over top. Sprinkle with caster sugar. Place under a very hot grill until sugar caramelizes. Serve at once.
Serves 8

Orange Terrine

PIES, TARTS AND FLANS

Pastries, cheesecakes, strudels or sweet flans – these cut-and-come-again desserts make for effortless entertaining.

Strawberry Cheesecake Slice

125g (4oz) plain flour

60g (2oz) butter

1 egg yolk

3 tblspn lemon juice

250g (8oz) ricotta cheese

125ml (4fl oz) natural low fat yogurt

2 eggs

2 tblspn lemon juice

60g (2oz) sugar

250g (8oz) strawberries, hulled and sliced

155ml (5fl oz) double cream, whipped

1 Preheat oven to 190°C (375°F/ Gas 5). Sift the flour into a bowl. Rub in the butter. Add the egg yolk and lemon juice, with a little cold water if required, to make a soft dough. Knead on a lightly floured surface until smooth, then press the dough evenly over the bottom of a 23cm (9in) springform cake tin. Cover loosely with greaseproof paper and baking beans. Bake blind for 8 minutes, remove the paper and beans and return the pastry base to the oven for 8 minutes more. Cool. Reduce the oven temperature to 180°C (350°F/ Gas 4).

2 Beat the ricotta, yogurt, eggs, lemon juice and sugar in a bowl until smooth. Pour over the pastry base. Bake the cheesecake for 30 minutes or until set; cool.

3 Purée half the strawberries in a blender or food processor; sieve to remove the seeds. Spread the purée over the cheesecake, then decorate with the whipped cream and remaining strawberries. Serve.

Serves 6-8

Pumpkin Pie

1 x 215g (7½oz) packet frozen shortcrust pastry, thawed

750g (1½lb) pumpkin, peeled, seeded and chopped

¼ tspn each ground cinnamon, cloves, ginger and grated nutmeg

2 eggs, separated

300ml (10fl oz) single cream

60ml (2fl oz) milk

185ml (6fl oz) clear honey

1 Preheat oven to 200°C (400°F/ Gas 6). Roll out the pastry on a floured board. Line a 23cm (9in) pie plate; use the pastry trimmings to decorate the rim.

2 Cook the pumpkin in a saucepan of salted boiling water until tender. Drain well.

3 Combine the cooked pumpkin, spices, eggs, cream, milk and honey in a blender or food processor. Process until smooth.

4 Pour the filling into the pastry case. Bake for 15 minutes, then lower the temperature to 180°C (350°F/Gas 4) and cook for 45 minutes more or until set. Serve warm, with cream or crème fraîche.

Serves 6

Variation

90g (3oz) soft brown sugar may be used instead of the honey, if preferred.

Strawberry Cheesecake Slice

Almond Caramel Tart

60g (2oz) butter

250g (8oz) golden syrup

2 tblspn brandy

2 eggs plus 2 egg yolks

250g (8oz) flaked almonds

Sweet Shortcrust Pastry

315g (10oz) plain flour

1 tblspn caster sugar

220g (7oz) cold butter, cut into small cubes

1 Preheat oven to 190°C (375°F/ Gas 5). Make pastry. Combine flour with sugar in a large bowl. Rub in butter until mixture resembles breadcrumbs. Add just enough iced water to hold pastry together. Quickly knead it into a ball, wrap and refrigerate for 30 minutes.

2 Roll out pastry to fit a 25cm (10in) flan tin. Line with grease-proof paper and add baking beans. Bake blind for 10 minutes, then remove paper and beans and bake for 5 minutes more. Set aside. Reduce oven temperature to 180°C (350°F/Gas 4).

3 For filling, melt butter with syrup and brandy in a saucepan over moderate heat. Cool slightly, then whisk in the beaten eggs and egg yolks. Sprinkle the almonds evenly over the pie shell, top with the syrup mixture and bake for 25-30 minutes.
Serves 8

Apple and Pear Pie

Apple and Pear Pie

1 x 375g (12oz) packet frozen shortcrust pastry, thawed

500g (1lb) Bramley apples, peeled, cored and thinly sliced

2 x 425g (13¹/₂oz) cans pears, drained and sliced

2 tblspn lemon juice

4 tblspn soft brown sugar

1 tspn ground cloves

1 tspn ground mixed spice

1 egg yolk

1 Preheat oven to 200°C (400°F/ Gas 6). Roll out half the pastry on a floured surface; line a 23cm (9in) fluted flan tin.

2 Place the apples in a saucepan with just enough water to cover. Simmer until tender. Drain and mix with the pears, lemon juice, sugar and spices. Cool.

3 Spoon the filling into the pie shell. Roll out the remaining pastry to make a lid. Cut leaf shapes from the trimmings and attach them to the pie crust with a little of the egg yolk. Glaze the pie with the remaining yolk.

4 Bake for 10 minutes, then lower the oven temperature to 180°C (350°F/Gas 4) and bake for 20 minutes more. Serve at once.
Serves 6

Almond Caramel Tart

Pear and Cream Tart

5 cooking pears

2 tblspn lemon juice

5 tblspn caster sugar

90ml (3fl oz) single cream

2-3 drops almond essence

Pastry

250g (8oz) plain flour

pinch salt

125g (4oz) cold butter, cubed

60g (2oz) caster sugar

1 egg yolk

1 Make the pastry. Combine the flour and salt in a bowl. Rub in the butter until the mixture resembles breadcrumbs, then stir in the sugar. Add the egg yolk with enough iced water to make a firm dough; wrap and refrigerate for 30 minutes.

2 Preheat oven to 200°C (400°F/ Gas 6). Roll out the pastry on a lightly floured surface to fit a 25cm (10in) pie tin. Place in the freezer for 20 minutes.

3 Meanwhile peel, core and halve the pears. Toss them with the lemon juice in a bowl, then arrange the pears cut side down in the pie shell. Sprinkle the sugar over the top. Bake for 20 minutes, until the pears begin to soften.

4 Mix the cream and almond essence together in a jug. Pour the mixture over the pears, return the tart to the oven and bake for 15 minutes more. Allow the tart to stand for 5-10 minutes before serving, with cream if liked.
Serves 8

Variation
Add an almond crumble topping to the tart to echo the almond essence in the cream. Put 185g (6oz) plain flour in a bowl; rub in 90g (3oz) butter and add 45g (1¹/₂oz) soft brown sugar. Stir in 90g (3oz) flaked almonds. Sprinkle the mixture over the tart after adding the cream mixture; bake for 30 minutes or until golden.

Walnut Apple Strudel

500g (1lb) Bramley apples, peeled, cored and thinly sliced

2 tblspn lemon juice

30g (1oz) walnuts, chopped

1 tblspn natural low fat yogurt

60g (2oz) sugar

1 tspn ground cinnamon

4 sheets filo pastry

60g (2oz) butter, melted

beaten egg for glazing

1 Toss the apple slices in the lemon juice in a bowl. Drain off the excess liquid. Stir in the walnuts, yogurt, sugar and cinnamon. Chill for 20 minutes.

2 Preheat oven to 180°C (350°F/ Gas 4). Keeping the rest of the filo covered with a clean tea-towel, place one sheet on the work surface. Brush it with the melted butter. Place a second sheet of filo on top of the first and brush with butter again. Repeat until all the filo has been used.

3 Place the filling along one long edge of the pastry, leaving a clear 5cm (2in) border where necessary so that the pastry can be turned in and rolled up like a long sausage. Roll the strudel, brush with the beaten egg and place on a lightly greased baking sheet. It may be necessary to curve the strudel into a horseshoe shape.

4 Bake the strudel for about 50 minutes or until golden. Serve sliced, warm or at room temperature, with clotted cream or crème fraîche.
Serves 6

Variation
Make the strudel with mincemeat, or with a mixture of mincemeat and apple, for a variation on traditional mince pies. Serve with brandy butter.

Rum Fig Tart

Rum Fig Tart

15-20 glacé figs
3 tblspn fig jam or marmalade
125ml (4fl oz) rum

Pastry

185g (6oz) plain flour
90g (3oz) butter, cut into small cubes
1 tblspn caster sugar
1 egg
2-3 tblspn chilled white wine

1 Make the pastry. Put the flour in a mixing bowl. Rub in the butter until the mixture resembles fine breadcrumbs. Stir in the caster sugar. Add the egg, with enough of the wine to make a dough; knead lightly. Wrap the dough and set it aside in a cool place for 30 minutes.

2 Preheat oven to 200°C (400°F/ Gas 6). Roll out the pastry thinly on a lightly floured surface to fit a 23cm (9in) flan tin. Line the pastry shell with greaseproof paper and add baking beans. Bake blind for 10 minutes, then remove the paper and beans, return the pastry shell to the oven and bake for 10 minutes more or until golden. Cool.

3 Arrange the figs in the pastry shell. In a small saucepan, heat the jam or marmalade with the rum until thin and syrupy. Brush the figs with the syrup. Decorate with mint sprigs. Serve with whipped cream, if liked.

Serves 6-8

Variation
Spread a layer of pastry cream in the cooked pastry shell before adding the figs, if liked: Whisk 2 egg yolks with 60g (2oz) caster sugar and 30g (1oz) plain flour in a bowl. Gradually add 300ml (10fl oz) hot milk, beating constantly. Pour the mixture into a saucepan and stir over low heat until the custard is thick, smooth and shiny. Cover closely and allow to cool before use.

Apple Slice

125g (4oz) self-raising flour

140g (4¹/₂oz) cornflour

110g (3¹/₂oz) butter, softened

90g (3oz) soft brown sugar

2 eggs, beaten

60g (2oz) caster sugar

3 Bramley apples, peeled, cored and grated

icing sugar for dusting

1 Preheat oven to 180°C (350°F/ Gas 4). Mix the flour and cornflour together. Beat the butter with the brown sugar in a bowl until creamy. Stir in the flour mixture alternately with the beaten eggs. Mix well.

2 Spread half the mixture evenly over the bottom of a greased 30 x 20cm (12 x 8in) cake tin. Sprinkle with the caster sugar.

3 Mix the apples with the remaining cake mixture. Spread the mixture carefully over the base layer in the tin.

4 Bake for 25-30 minutes. Cool the cake in the tin, then dust the surface with icing sugar. Cut into slices and serve, with whipped cream and sliced strawberries if liked.
Makes 12

Lemon Chiffon Pie

250g (8oz) golden oatmeal biscuits

75g (2¹/₂oz) butter, melted

125ml (4fl oz) lemon juice

4 eggs, separated

grated rind of 1 lemon

185g (6oz) caster sugar

2 tspn powdered gelatine

60ml (2fl oz) white wine

1 Crush the biscuits in a food processor, or place them in a stout polythene bag and crush them with a rolling pin. Mix with the melted butter. Press the mixture onto the bottom and sides of a greased 20cm (8in) springform cake tin. Refrigerate until firm.

2 Bring lemon juice to the boil in a saucepan. Meanwhile, using a hand-held electric mixer, beat the egg yolks with the lemon rind and 125g (4oz) of the caster sugar in a large bowl. Add the boiling lemon juice in a steady stream, beating constantly.

3 Dissolve the gelatine in the wine (see page 5); stir into the egg yolk mixture.

4 Beat the egg whites in a grease-free bowl until stiff. Gradually beat in the remaining sugar; beat for 3 minutes more. Fold into the lemon mixture. Pour filling into biscuit crust. Chill until set.
Serves 6

Topsy-turvy Pear Tart

155g (5oz) plain flour

185g (6oz) butter

1 tblspn caster sugar

2 tblspn iced water

2 tblspn finely chopped fresh mint

2 tblspn soft brown sugar

4 pears, peeled, halved and cored

1 Put the flour in a mixing bowl. Cut 125g (4oz) of the butter into small cubes, add to the flour and rub in until the mixture resembles fine breadcrumbs. Stir in the caster sugar. Add enough iced water to make a dough; wrap and set aside in a cool place for 30 minutes.

2 Preheat oven to 190°C (375°F/ Gas 5). Melt the remaining butter in a small pan; pour into a 20cm (8in) pie dish. Sprinkle with mint and brown sugar. Arrange the pears, core side uppermost, on top.

3 Roll out the pastry on a floured surface. Cut a circle to exactly fit the dish. Gently place the pastry on top of the pears. Bake for 15-20 minutes until golden. Cool in the dish for 20 minutes. Invert on a plate to serve.
Serves 8

Topsy-turvy Pear Tart

Apple Slice

Glacé Fig Orange Tart

Glacé Fig Orange Tart

220g (7oz) butter

250g (8oz) digestive biscuits, crushed

315g (10oz) glacé figs, chopped

250ml (8fl oz) frozen concentrated orange juice, thawed

2 eggs, lightly beaten

30g (1oz) pinenuts

1 Preheat oven to 180°C (350°F/ Gas 4). Melt 125g (4oz) butter; combine with biscuit crumbs to make a 23cm (9in) pie shell (see Lemon Chiffon Pie, page 34).

2 Simmer figs and orange juice together in a frying pan for 15 minutes. Off the heat, stir in remaining butter. Cool for 5 minutes.

3 Quickly stir eggs into fig mixture. Pour into crumb crust. Sprinkle with nuts. Bake for 20 minutes.

Serves 4-6

Treacle Tart

1 x 215g (7oz) packet frozen puff pastry, thawed

60g (2oz) fresh white breadcrumbs

185g (6oz) golden syrup

grated rind and juice of 1/2 lemon

1 tblspn dark rum

1 Preheat oven to 180°C (350°F/ Gas 4). Roll out pastry on a lightly floured surface to fit a 20cm (8in) loose-based pie tin. Reserve the pastry trimmings.

2 Combine remaining ingredients; mix well and pour into pastry shell. Reroll pastry trimmings and cut into 1cm (1/2in) strips. Twist strips and make a lattice design on top of filling.

3 Bake for 50 minutes or until pastry is golden brown. Cool on a wire rack. Serve lukewarm.

Serves 6-8

Nutty Date Tart

3 eggs, separated

185g (6oz) sugar

315g (10oz) pitted dates, chopped

125g (4oz) walnuts, roughly chopped

2 tblspn plain flour

2 tspn ground cinnamon

clotted cream to serve

1 Preheat oven to 160°C (325°F/ Gas 3). Beat egg yolks with sugar until pale and creamy.

2 Combine dates, walnuts and flour in a bowl. Sprinkle with half the cinnamon. Pour over egg yolk mixture and mix well.

3 Beat egg whites in a bowl until stiff peaks form. Fold into date mixture. Pour into a greased baking dish and sprinkle with remaining cinnamon. Bake for 45 minutes, cool to room temperature and serve with cream.

Serves 6

Peach Tart

Apple Flan with Apricot Calvados Glaze

125g (4oz) plain flour

4 tblspn cornflour

155g (5oz) butter, chopped

2 Bramley apples, peeled, cored and sliced

185g (6oz) apricot jam

2 tblspn Calvados

1 Preheat oven to 190°C (375°F/ Gas 5). Combine the flour and cornflour in a mixing bowl. Rub in the butter until the mixture resembles fine breadcrumbs. Add enough cold water to form a dough. Knead lightly, wrap and set aside for 30 minutes in a cool place.

2 Roll out the pastry on a lightly floured surface to fit a 20cm (8in) flan tin. Line the pie shell with greaseproof paper and add baking beans. Bake blind for 10 minutes, then remove the paper and beans.

Reduce the oven temperature to 180°C (350°F/Gas 4).

3 Arrange apples in concentric circles in pastry case. In a medium saucepan, melt the jam with the Calvados over low heat.

4 Brush the apples with the jam mixture. Bake for 30-35 minutes or until the pie shell is golden and the apples are cooked and glazed. Serve hot or cold, with custard, cream or crème fraîche.
Serves 6

Variation
Use redcurrant jelly and port for the glaze, if preferred.

Peach Tart

1 x 375g (12oz) packet frozen shortcrust pastry, thawed

2 large peaches, skinned, halved and pitted

6 tblspn peach jam, melted

1 Preheat oven to 180°C (350°F/ Gas 4). Roll out the pastry on a lightly floured surface and cut out a 23cm (9in) round. Reroll the remaining pastry and cut 1cm (1/2in) strips. Place the pastry round on a baking sheet; using a pastry brush, lightly moisten the edge with water.

2 Gently press a strip of pastry around the edge of the round, shaping it with your fingertips. Continue with the remaining strips to build up about 6 layers in all.

3 Slice the peaches very finely. Spread two thirds of the jam over the bottom of the pastry shell. Overlap the peach slices on top and brush with the remaining jam. Bake for 20 minutes. Serve warm.
Serves 8

Rhubarb Tatin

500g (1lb) rhubarb, trimmed and sliced

155g (5oz) soft brown sugar

pinch of ground cinnamon

2 eggs

3 tblspn single cream

2 tblspn plain flour

icing sugar to taste

Pastry

125g (4oz) plain flour

pinch salt

60g (2oz) chilled butter, diced

1 tblspn caster sugar

1 egg yolk, lightly beaten

1/4 tspn vanilla essence

4-5 tblspn iced water

1 Preheat oven to 230°C (450°F/ Gas 8). Place the rhubarb in an ovenproof dish, sprinkle with the brown sugar and cinnamon and mix well. Bake for 20 minutes. Lower the oven temperature to 180°C (350°F/Gas 4).

2 Transfer the rhubarb mixture to a greased 23cm (9in) flan dish. Beat the eggs, cream and flour in a bowl; spread the mixture over the rhubarb.

3 Make the pastry. Combine the flour and salt in a mixing bowl. Rub in the butter until the mixture resembles breadcrumbs. Add the caster sugar, egg yolk and vanilla, with enough of the iced water to make a soft dough. Knead lightly.

4 On a floured surface, roll out the dough to a round large enough to fit the flan dish very comfortably. Place on top of the rhubarb, gently pressing the pastry inside the edges where possible.

5 Make a slit in the pastry to allow steam to escape. Bake for 30 minutes or until the pastry crust is golden brown. Cool in the dish for 10 minutes, then invert onto a serving plate. Dust with icing sugar before serving.
Serves 6-8

Caramel Apple Pie

315g (10oz) plain flour

220g (7oz) butter, chilled

1 tblspn caster sugar

220g (7oz) soft brown sugar

60ml (2fl oz) water

1 x 397g (12½ oz) can condensed milk

250ml (8fl oz) double cream

4 egg yolks, beaten

2 Bramley apples, peeled, cored and sliced

1 Put the flour in a mixing bowl. Cut the butter into cubes, add to the flour and rub in until the mixture resembles breadcrumbs. Add the caster sugar, then stir in enough iced water to form a dough. Knead quickly, wrap and set aside in a cool place for 30 minutes.

2 Preheat oven to 190°C (375°F/ Gas 5). Roll out the pastry on a floured surface to fit a 25cm (10in) flan tin. Line with greaseproof paper and baking beans and bake blind for 10 minutes. Remove paper and beans and bake for 5 minutes more.

3 Heat 185g (6oz) of the brown sugar with the water in a small pan. Stir until the sugar has dissolved, then boil without stirring until the mixture thickens to a toffee-like consistency. Cool for 5 minutes.

4 Whisk in the condensed milk and cream, cook for 5 minutes, then whisk in the egg yolks. Pour into the pie shell and bake for 20 minutes; cool to room temperature.

5 Meanwhile, cook the apples with a little water in a saucepan until softened, but still retaining their shape. Drain thoroughly. Arrange on top of the pie. Sprinkle with the remaining brown sugar and place under a hot grill for just long enough to caramelize the sugar. Serve warm, decorated with whipped cream and cinnamon, if liked.
Serves 6-8

Glazed Fruit Tart

315g (10oz) plain flour

220g (7oz) chilled butter, cubed

1 tblspn caster sugar

375ml (12fl oz) carton custard

155ml (5fl oz) double cream

2 tspn powdered gelatine

60ml (2fl oz) orange juice

2 tblspn Cointreau

2 kiwi fruit, peeled, sliced and halved

125g (4oz) drained cooked cranberries

1 large peach, skinned, halved, pitted and thinly sliced

1 passionfruit

90g (3oz) smooth apricot jam

1 Put the flour in a mixing bowl. Rub in the butter until the mixture resembles breadcrumbs, stir in the caster sugar, then add enough iced water to make a dough. Knead lightly, wrap and set aside in a cool place for 30 minutes.

2 Preheat oven to 190°C (375°F/ Gas 5). Roll out the pastry on a floured surface to fit a 25cm (10in) flan dish. Line with greaseproof paper and baking beans and bake blind for 10 minutes. Remove paper and beans and bake for 5 minutes more. Cool.

3 Mix the custard with the cream in a bowl. Dissolve the gelatine in the orange juice (see page 5). Cool, then stir into the custard cream mixture. Stir in the Cointreau.

4 Pour the flavoured custard cream into the cold pie shell, levelling it neatly. Refrigerate for about 30 minutes or until set.

5 Decorate the top of the tart with the fruit as shown in the photograph. Melt the jam in a small saucepan; brush it over the top of the fruit to glaze. Set the tart aside for 30 minutes before serving.
Serves 8

Caramel Apple Pie, Glazed Fruit Tart

ICES

Scoop all rivals in the sweet stakes with these sensational treats. Mango Ice Cream, Coffee Granita, Strawberry Ice and Lemon Tequila Sorbet are just some of the delights on ice.

Lemon Tequila Sorbet

375g (12oz) sugar

275ml (9fl oz) water

1 tblspn powdered gelatine

5 tblspn lemon juice

5 tblspn tequila

1 tblspn finely grated lemon rind

250ml (8fl oz) evaporated milk

1 Combine the sugar and 250ml (8fl oz) of the water in a small saucepan. Bring to the boil, stirring until the sugar has dissolved, then boil without stirring for 5 minutes.

2 Dissolve the gelatine in the remaining water (see page 5). Stir the mixture into the hot syrup.

3 Add the lemon juice, tequila and lemon rind to the syrup. Cool, stir in the evaporated milk and pour the mixture into a bowl. Chill for 1 hour.

4 Pour the mixture into an ice cream maker and chill according to instructions. Alternatively, freeze in ice trays. When semi-frozen, beat the mixture in a bowl to break up any large ice crystals. Repeat the process twice more, then freeze in a suitable container until solid.
Serves 6-8

Apricot and Raspberry Yogurt Ice

300ml (10fl oz) natural low fat yogurt

2 tblspn clear honey

185g (6oz) drained canned apricots

185g (6oz) raspberries, hulled

1 Combine the yogurt and honey in a freezerproof bowl. Freeze until firm.

2 Purée the apricots with the raspberries in a blender or food processor. Press through a sieve to remove the raspberry seeds, then return the purée to the blender or food processor. Add the frozen yogurt and blend until smooth. Return to the freezer until set, or freeze in an ice-cream maker.
Serves 4

Yogurt Passionfruit Ice Cream

2 tblspn clear honey

215ml (7fl oz) natural low fat yogurt

1 tspn powdered gelatine

2 tblspn water

1 egg white

pulp of 1 passionfruit, plus extra to decorate

1 Combine the honey and yogurt in a bowl; mix well. Dissolve the gelatine in the water (see page 5). Cool slightly, then stir into the yogurt mixture. Freeze in ice trays until firm.

2 Transfer the frozen yogurt mixture to a large bowl. Using a hand-held electric mixer, beat until the mixture doubles in bulk.

3 Beat the egg white in a grease-free bowl until stiff peaks form. Fold into the yogurt mixture with the passionfruit pulp. Freeze in a freezerproof container until firm. Decorate with passionfruit pulp.
Serves 4

Yogurt Passionfruit Ice Cream

Chocolate Brandy Ice Cream

750ml (1¼pt) double cream

250ml (8fl oz) milk

155g (5oz) dark chocolate, grated

2 tspn instant coffee powder

5 egg yolks

185g (6oz) caster sugar

2 tblspn brandy

1 Combine the cream, milk, chocolate and coffee in a large saucepan over moderate heat. Stir until the chocolate melts, do not allow mixture to boil.

2 Meanwhile, using an electric mixer, beat egg yolks with sugar until pale and thick. Continue to beat while adding hot mocha cream. Return mixture to a clean pan and stir constantly over moderate heat until mixture thickens slightly. Stir in brandy. Set aside until cool.

3 Pour mixture into an ice cream maker and chill according to instructions. Alternatively, freeze in ice trays. When semi-frozen, beat mixture to break up any large ice crystals. Repeat the process twice more, then freeze in a suitable container until solid.
Serves 12

Coffee Ice Cream with Walnuts and Lychees

125g (4oz) walnuts

12 scoops good quality coffee ice cream

6 tblspn clear honey

375g (12oz) freshly peeled lychees

1 Preheat oven to 180°C (350°F/ Gas 4). Spread out walnuts on a baking sheet; toast in oven for about 10 minutes or until golden. Cool.

2 Place 2 scoops of coffee ice cream in each serving dish. Drizzle with honey, add a few lychees and sprinkle with toasted walnuts. Add a little rum or Tia Maria just before serving, if liked.
Serves 6

Strawberry Ice

Strawberry Ice

315g (10oz) cantaloupe melon flesh, chopped

185g (6oz) strawberries, hulled

2 tblspn lemon juice

60g (2oz) sugar

125ml (4fl oz) water

1 Purée melon, strawberries, lemon juice, sugar and water in a blender or food processor.

2 Pour mixture into an ice cream maker and chill according to instructions. Alternatively, freeze in ice trays. When semi-frozen, beat the mixture to break up any large ice crystals. Repeat the process twice more, then freeze in a suitable container until solid.
Serves 6

Quick Choc-Chip Ice Cream

250ml (8fl oz) double cream

3 tblspn Kahlua

2 litres (3½pt) good quality vanilla ice cream, softened

250g (8oz) chocolate chips

125g (4oz) almonds, chopped

1 Whip cream with Kahlua until soft peaks form; fold mixture into ice cream. Spoon into a freezerproof container and freeze until semi-frozen.

2 Beat mixture to break up any large ice crystals. Stir in chocolate chips and nuts. Freeze until solid.
Serves 12

Frozen Cream Bombe

500ml (16fl oz) double cream

2 tblspn Cointreau

3 tblspn finely grated lemon rind

220g (7oz) coconut macaroons, crushed

2 tblspn caster sugar

2 tblspn lemon juice

175ml (6fl oz) freshly squeezed orange juice

1 tblspn orange marmalade

1 tspn cornflour

1 tblspn water

1 Whip cream in a bowl until soft peaks form. Stir in Cointreau and lemon rind. Fold macaroons into cream mixture.

2 Spoon mixture into a lightly oiled 1 litre (1³/₄pt) bombe mould. Cover. Freeze overnight.

3 Make the sauce. Combine sugar, lemon juice, orange juice and marmalade in a saucepan. Heat gently until mixture boils. Mix cornflour to a paste with water. Stir into sauce. Cook, stirring constantly, until sauce thickens. Serve warm, with the sliced bombe.

Serves 8

Mango Ice Cream

2 x 439g (14oz) cans sliced mangoes, drained

4 tblspn lemon juice

185g (6oz) caster sugar

2 eggs, separated

300ml (10fl oz) double cream, whipped

1 Set aside a few mango slices for decoration. Purée mango with lemon juice and caster sugar in a blender or food processor. Transfer to a bowl. Cover. Refrigerate.

2 Using an electric mixer, beat egg yolks until pale and creamy. In a separate bowl, beat egg whites until stiff.

3 Fold egg yolks into cream, then fold in mango purée. Finally, fold in stiffly beaten egg whites.

4 Spoon mixture into an ice cream maker and chill according to instructions. Alternatively, freeze in ice trays. When semi-frozen, beat the mixture to break up any large ice crystals. Repeat the process once more, then freeze in a suitable container until solid.

5 Soften slightly before serving, decorated with strawberries and the reserved mango slices.

Serves 4-6

Mango Ice Cream

Frozen Nutty Choc Terrine

300g (9¹/₂oz) milk chocolate

250g (8oz) chocolate and hazelnut spread

60ml (2fl oz) Tia Maria

6 eggs, separated

600ml (1pt) double cream

3 tblspn caster sugar

250g (8oz) dark chocolate

1 In a large heatproof bowl, melt milk chocolate with the chocolate and hazelnut spread (see Kitchen Tip, page 19). Cool slightly, stir in Tia Maria and egg yolks. Whip half the cream until soft peaks form; fold into chocolate mixture.

2 Beat egg whites in a bowl until soft peaks form. Gradually add sugar, beating until mixture is stiff.

3 Melt dark chocolate; fold half into creamy chocolate mixture, then fold in the egg whites. Keep remaining chocolate warm over hot water.

4 Spoon mixture into a large loaf tin lined with cling film. Freeze until firm.

5 Make sauce by adding the remaining cream to the reserved chocolate. Stir over low heat until smooth. Serve with the sliced terrine.

Serves 12

Hazelnut Ice Cream

500ml (16fl oz) milk

110g (3¹/₂oz) hazelnuts, ground

250ml (8fl oz) double cream

2 tspn vanilla essence

6 egg yolks

185g (6oz) soft brown sugar

Frozen Nutty Choc Terrine

Coffee Granita, Hazelnut Ice Cream

1 Bring milk to the boil in a saucepan. Stir in hazelnuts, cream and vanilla; lower the heat to a bare simmer.

2 Beat egg yolks with sugar until pale and creamy. Gradually add two thirds of the milk mixture, beating constantly.

3 Pour the contents of the mixing bowl into the remaining milk mixture in the pan. Cook over moderate heat, stirring constantly, until the mixture thickens enough to coat the back of a spoon. Cool.

4 Pour mixture into an ice cream maker and freeze according to instructions. Alternatively, freeze in ice trays. When semi-frozen, beat the mixture to break up any large ice crystals. Repeat the process twice more, then freeze in a suitable container until solid.

Serves 6

Coffee Granita

125g (4oz) sugar

750ml (1¼pt) strong black coffee

½ tspn ground cinnamon

½ tspn ground mixed spice

2 tblspn Tia Maria

mint sprigs to decorate

1 Combine sugar, coffee, cinnamon, mixed spice and Tia Maria in a saucepan. Heat, stirring until sugar dissolves, then boil without stirring for 2 minutes.

2 When cool, pour mixture into a freezerproof container. Freeze for 3 hours, then beat the mixture to break up the ice crystals. Repeat the process once more, then freeze until solid.

3 Transfer granita to refrigerator 15 minutes before serving. Stir with a fork to break up ice, spoon into dessert glasses and decorate with mint.

Serves 4-6

Yogurt Orange Ice Cream

Yogurt Orange Ice Cream

4 tblspn clear honey

375ml (12fl oz) orange-flavoured yogurt

1 tblspn powdered gelatine

60ml (2fl oz) water

1 tspn vanilla essence

2 tspn finely grated orange rind

2 tblspn freshly squeezed orange juice

2 egg whites

1 Combine the honey and yogurt in a large bowl; mix well. Dissolve the gelatine in the water (see page 5). Cool slightly, then stir into the yogurt mixture.

2 Line a loaf tin with cling film. Spoon the yogurt mixture into the tin, cover and freeze for 3 hours.

3 Beat the frozen mixture in a large bowl until doubled in bulk. Beat in the vanilla, orange rind and juice.

4 Whisk the egg whites to soft peaks in a separate, grease-free bowl. Fold into the yogurt ice, return the mixture to the loaf tin, cover and freeze until solid. Soften slightly before serving, with fresh fruit, if liked.

Serves 6-8

Pear Ice Cream

90ml (3fl oz) lemon juice

60ml (2fl oz) water

185g (6oz) sugar

3 firm, ripe pears, peeled, halved, cored and diced

250ml (8fl oz) double cream

250ml (8fl oz) milk

1 Combine the lemon juice, water and sugar in a saucepan. Heat, stirring until all the sugar has dissolved. Add the pears and simmer for 8 minutes. Remove the pan from the heat and allow the pears to steep in the mixture for 5 minutes more.

2 Transfer the warm pears and liquid to a blender or food processor. Purée until smooth, stopping once to scrape down the sides with a spatula. With the machine running, add the cream and milk through the feeder tube and process for just long enough to combine.

3 Pour the mixture into an ice cream maker and freeze according to instructions. Alternatively, freeze in ice trays. When semi-frozen, beat the mixture in a bowl to break up any large ice crystals. Repeat the process twice more, then freeze in a suitable container until solid.

Serves 6

Useful Information

Length

Centimetres	Inches	Centimetres	Inches
0.5 (5mm)	$1/4$	18	7
1	$1/2$	20	8
2	$3/4$	23	9
2.5	1	25	10
4	$1^{1}/2$	30	12
5	2	35	14
6	$2^{1}/2$	40	16
7.5	3	45	18
10	4	50	20
15	6	NB: 1cm = 10mm	

Metric/Imperial Conversion Chart
Mass (Weight)
(Approximate conversions for cookery purposes)

Metric	Imperial	Metric	Imperial
15g	$1/2$oz	315g	10oz
30g	1oz	350g	11oz
60g	2oz	375g	12oz ($3/4$lb)
90g	3oz	410g	13oz
125g	4oz ($1/4$lb)	440g	14oz
155g	5oz	470g	15oz
185g	6oz	500g (0.5kg)	16oz (1lb)
220g	7oz	750g	24oz ($1^{1}/2$lb)
250g	8oz ($1/2$lb)	1000g (1kg)	32oz (2lb)
280g	9oz	1500 (1.5kg)	3lb

Metric Spoon Sizes

$1/4$ teaspoon = 1.25ml	
$1/2$ teaspoon = 2.5ml	
1 teaspoon = 5ml	
1 tablespoon =15ml	

Liquids

Metric	Imperial
30ml	1fl oz
60ml	2fl oz
90ml	3fl oz
125ml	4fl oz
155ml	5fl oz ($1/4$pt)
185ml	6fl oz
250ml	8fl oz
500ml	16fl oz
600ml	20fl oz (1pt)
750ml	$1^{1}/4$pt
1 litre	$1^{3}/4$pt
1.2 litres	2pt
1.5 litres	$2^{1}/2$pt
1.8 litres	3pt
2 litres	$3^{1}/2$pt
2.5 litres	4pt

Index

Editorial Coordination: Merehurst Limited
Cookery Editor: Jenni Fleetwood
Editorial Assistant: Sheridan Packer
Production Managers: Sheridan Carter, Anna Maguire
Layout and Finished Art: Stephen Joesph
Cover Photography: David Gill
Cover Design: Maggie Aldred
Cover Home Economist: Liz Trigg
Cover Stylist: Hilary Guy

Published by J.B. Fairfax Press Pty Limited
80-82 McLachlan Avenue
Rushcutters Bay 2011
A.C.N. 003 738 430

Formatted by J. B. Fairfax Press Pty Limited
Printed by Toppan Printing Co, Singapore

JBFP 320 A/UK
Includes Index
ISBN 1 86343 116 0 (set)
ISBN 1 86343 159 4

Distribution and Sales Enquiries
Australia: J.B. Fairfax Press Pty Limited
Ph: (02) 361 6366 Fax: (02) 360 6262
United Kingdom: J.B. Fairfax Press Pty Limited
Ph: (0933) 402330 Fax: (0933) 402234